Coaching The Modern 4-2-3-1 Soccer Formation
Tactical Essentials & Training Exercises

By Marcus DiBernardo

Table of Contents

Introduction

The 4-2-3-1 is a system my college team has been playing for years. At the professional level, Arsenal, Real Madrid, Everton, Bayern Munich and many more have also been using this system effectively for the past few years. The formation is comprised of four lines compared to the typical three lines of most formations. This helps create many passing options between lines when in possession and allows for good compactness when defending.

One of the things I like the most about the 4-2-3-1 is the potential for movement off the ball when in possession. The attacking team can create problems for the defending team through the inter-changing of positions, playing in between the lines and creating overloads in the area of the ball. The defending team will be forced to problem solve and resist being dragged out of position.

The 4-2-3-1 can be employed in many different ways depending on the personnel available. Opening up the field and playing a possession-oriented game in the opponent's attacking third with a slow back four may not be advisable. In today's fast paced counter attack game, a high back line that lacks pace might be inviting trouble. However, the beauty of the formation is that it can be adapted to the personnel and employed in many different ways. The 4-2-3-1 can be used to play a conservative, defensively sound counter-attacking system or opened up for an ultra offensive system.

The difference between formations in soccer is simply a matter of about 10 yards in player positioning. A 4-3-3, 4-4-2, 4-5-1 & 4-2-3-1 are actually all very similar and difficult to identify once the game has started. The transition from defending to attacking creates a totally new shape and seemingly a new formation. The coach will add tactical guidelines for executing the formation. These may include a line of restraint, line of confrontation, pressing, zonal pressing, areas to exploit off the counter attack and more. All these tactical objectives will directly influence the way the 4-2-3-1 is played. The flexibility in the system allows for instant game management solutions. Going a goal up with 5 minutes to play may mean the wingbacks stop pushing forward in attack and the wingers drop deeper to defend. The interchanging of positions, room for tactical adjustments, defensive soundness, room for creativity and overall fluidity of the system is what makes the 4-2-3-1 effective and enjoyable to play and coach. This book will take you through the fundamental roles and responsibilities of the system to movement patterns, team defending, team attacking, training drills and tactical modifications. I hope you enjoy the book and feel free to email me with any questions you may have at coachdibernardo@gmail.com

The Numbering System for Player Identification

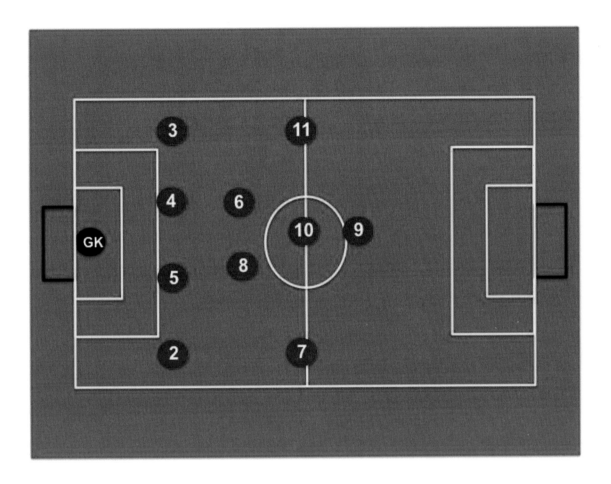

#1 (GK) – Goalkeeper
#2 – Right Wing Back
#3 – Left Wing Back
#4 – Left Center Back
#5 – Right Center Back
#6 – Defensive Center Midfielder
#8 – Passing Center Midfielder
#10 – Attacking Center Midfielder
#11 – Left Wing
#7 – Right Wing
#9 – Forward

Individual Player Roles & Responsibilities

Wing Backs - #2 & #3

In modern soccer the wingbacks (fullbacks) must be some of the fittest players on the field. Gone are the days when the fullbacks were slower and not expected to get up and down the field. The modern wingback is expected to have the characteristics of a pure winger and cover just as much ground. Along with the physical and technical demands the wingback must also possess a strong soccer IQ. The wingback must understand when to surge forward, when to underlap or overlap, be able to recognize and create attacking overloads, be calm in possession, possess 1v1 ability, have an excellent passing range, be an accurate crosser of the ball, must be willing to work hard for the team and be accountable for all defensive responsibilities.

Playing the 4-2-3-1 will often require the wingbacks to get forward and join the attack. These forward runs will create attacking overloads and match-up/marking problems for the defense to solve. Most of us will not have the chance to coach a wingback who possesses all these qualities, so tactically we must set our wing backs up for success by playing to their strengths and minimizing their weaknesses. In training, the coach can work on the player's weaknesses to make them into strengths. The wingbacks role in the 4-2-3-1 is instrumental to the success of the system. The relationship between the wingback and the winger is very important in terms of understanding each other's movements. Collective team attacking movements require players understand how to create space, the importance of timing runs, defenders & teammates positioning and how to create overloads in attack.

Strong in air, tackle – attacking 50% - defending 50% - must build great relationship with winger and center back on his side.

Center Backs - #4 & #5

The center backs must be able to defend 1v1, organize the team from the back and play safe passes; they must also understand zonal and man marking, where to set the line of restraint, when to push, hold or drop the line, be dominant in the air and have excellent sprinting speed. This is not an easy position to play. There is a shortage of quality center backs even at the highest level of soccer. A team that plays deeper and looks to counter attack can accommodate center backs with less speed. Teams that commit forward as a unit and stress possession must have center backs that can handle difficult 1v1 duals and are able to chase down longer balls over the top. Reading the play, anticipating and being intelligent do little in a 45-yard sprint for a ball into space. Recently, Tottenham, Arsenal and Manchester United have all been exposed for a lack of pace in the back. Often the best way to handle players that can hurt you with pace (like Cristiano Ronaldo) is to sit deeper and reduce the space they have to run into. When Brendon Rodgers was at Swansea City they possessed the ball, but they did it in their own defensive third and the middle third. They rarely gave their opponents the chance to exploit large amounts of space behind their back line. Knowing their center backs were skilled but not physically gifted they were able to possess the ball and limit their chances to be exploited with speed. At the same time, their opponents would come up the field, allowing Swansea to exploit that space.

Another way to make up for a slight lack of pace is to not have the center backs open up as wide while in possession. My advice is to consider the strengths and weaknesses of your center backs and put them in a position to succeed. The variables will not only include your team but the other team as well. If the forwards on the other team are lightening fast and provide a poor match-up, it would be time to consider adjustments in tactics.

Defensive Center Midfielder - #6

The defensive center mid is the pivot player that normally sits just in front of the two center backs. Physically this player should be powerful, fast and able to defend well. The defensive center mid should also have excellent long and short passing range to both sides of the field. Occasionally the defensive center mid can go forward as passing center mid would most likely cover for him. The #6 helps establish the tempo of the game and keeps the ball moving with simple, efficient and quick ball movement.

Central or Passing Center Midfielder - #8

This player must be physically strong possessing pace, power and endurance. The #8 serves as the ink between the defensive center mid and the attacking center mid. The defensive and attacking duties for this player are about equal. The #8 should be a good technical player, comfortable playing with back to play, have excellent passing range, have the ability to dictate the pace of the game, be willing to work hard for the team without the ball (ball winner) and be able to exploit the opponent's defense with penetrating passes or runs. The center midfield position requires a well-rounded player who has technique, intelligence and a physical presence. The #8 is really the engine of the team that helps drive the group. There is no hiding as a central midfielder. This position requires players to play hard and be accountable for all 90 minutes. The center mid must form a working relationship with the #6 and #10. The #6 will sit deeper most of the game as the #8 presents a passing option for the #6. The link from defensive center midfielder to the passing center midfielder in terms of ball possession is critical. The #10 or attacking center midfielder is the playmaker and serves as the main attacking partner for the #8. The passing center midfielder wants to get the ball into the #10 (attacking center midfielder) as much as possible. The partnership and understanding of roles and responsibilities between the #6,8 and 10 at midfielder is very important. The #8 can of course can hit penetrating passes to the wingers, wingbacks and even surge forward himself to score.

Attacking Center Midfielder - #10

The attacking midfielder must be a very good 1v1 player, have excellent vision for penetrating passing, be creative and unpredictable, be able to play quick combinations or shoot in tight spaces and always be considered a threat to score when on the ball. The #10 will inter-change positions frequently with the #9 (forward). The #10 will need to work effectively with the #9 and #8. The effectiveness of the #9 will be measured in goals and assists. However, the days of the attacking center mid walking around and not playing defense are over. Todays #10 is expected to work hard on the defensive side of the ball. That could be pressing in the attacking third when possession is lost or it could mean playing as part of the midfield unit helping to defend.

Wingers or Outside Midfielders - #7 & #11

Wingers in the modern game must be up and down the field defending and attacking. These players must possess speed, dribbling ability, technical ability, be good crossers of the ball and be willing to work hard for the team on defense. However, the modern winger is much than just a fast player that works hard up and down the sideline and crosses the ball. Today's winger must be good in possession and always looking to create overloads that can be exploited with intelligent combination play. Wingers often come into the center of the field allowing the outside wingbacks to come forward. Once the winger is central they must be able to play almost with the same skills as a central midfield player. The partnership between the winger (#7 & 11) and the wingback (#2 & #3) is very important. If the winger pushes inside the wingback takes the outside space. If the winger stays high and wide the wingback can under-lap.

Forward or Striker - #9

The 4-2-3-1 formation only employees one forward. This makes it essential that the player be able to hold the ball up under pressure. The #9 should be very fast with and without the ball, possess great 1v1 ability, be able to get into good scoring positions, be a good combination player, have an excellent shot and be a natural finisher. The forward (#9) and the attacking center midfielder (#10) must create an effective understanding/partnership between each other. The interchanging between the #9 and #10 will confuse the defense and open up spaces to play into.

I always liked my #9 to be extremely fast, so the counter attack is always available. Tall strong target forwards with average or below average pace limit the teams ability to break quickly on the counter.

Goalkeeper - #1 (GK – Used in Book)

Every coach wants the keeper to be well rounded possessing both skillful feet and hands. Ideally the keeper is a minimum of 6ft tall and athletic. I want my keeper to be a leader and organizer who literally directs the entire game from the goal. Keepers that read the game and direct their team can shut down dangerous situations before they even happen. Intelligent keepers can do everything from intercepting through-balls to starting a quick counter attack.

4-2-3-1 Phases of Play and Transitions

How many times do I hear a coach say "I think they are playing a 4-4-2 or I think they are playing a 4-3-3". The reality is, it's hard to tell what formation a team is playing during the flow of the game. The starting formation may only be recognizable before the whistle or in the defensive phase. Soccer is a free flowing game with the set-up of players constantly changing and moving. The teams defending shape may look like a 4-2-3-1, while the attacking shape may look like a 3-1-3-3 or 3-1-5-1. When a team loses possession or gains possession, a chain reaction of movements will follow. Coaches should understand each and every player's movement options and responsibilities from defending to attack and attack to defending. Once the coach has a firm understanding of the movements, he can create a game plan that will dictate the way the team will play. For example, if the coach wants to be more conservative, he can restrict the opposite side wingback from going forward. This will make the team more defensively sound, but it will limit wide attacking play on the far side. If the team is in need of a goal, the coach can push the two wingers high and limit how far they will drop while defending. All these adjustments change the shape of the team and alter the movement of players. <u>The main point is the same formation can be played many different ways with it's own strengths and weaknesses.</u> Coaches must study all aspects and phases of the formation and learn how and why to make adjustments. Great tactical coaches learn on the job. They are always observing, reflecting, adjusting and learning while watching the game.

The three phases below demonstrate the three basic team shapes of the 4-2-3-1 during a game. It is important to have an understanding of all three phases and the transitions between the phases. These are just examples as the shapes and movements can vary.

(Phase One) Defensive Shape: 4-2-3-1

This example shows the four lines as the team is in a compact shape. To make the team even more compact the #11 can drop in line next to the #6.

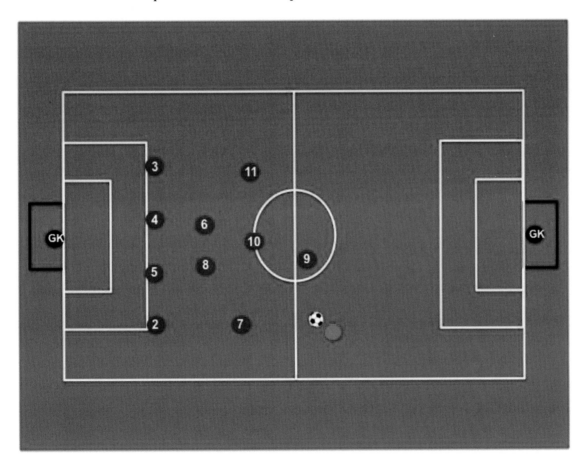

(Phase Two) Defensive & Middle Third in Possession: 3-3-1-3 or 3-3-1-2-1

The team gains possession in the defensive third as players start to open up in order to build possession. Teams can elect to build possession at this point or try and counter quickly with a direct pass. If the team builds possession their movements should open up the field stretching their opponents. Triangles and diamonds should start to be formed all over the field in terms of passing angles for the team in possession. Teams that struggle to keep possession will have a hard time transitioning from the defending phase to the attacking phase by building play up; they will be more likely to play direct.

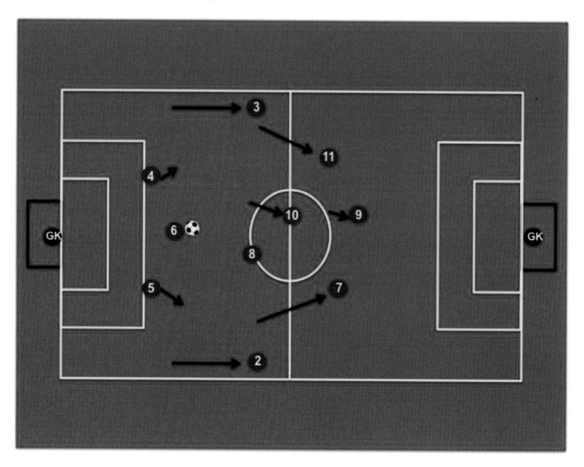

(Phase Three) Ultra Attacking in Attack Third in Possession: 3-1-5-1

In this example both wingbacks #2 & #3 are fully committed forward into attack.

The wingers #7 & #11 have made diagonal runs inside forming a diamond shape with

the #9 & #10. The defensive center midfielder #6 operates as the swingman while

providing defensive cover as an extra center back. The passing center mid #8 adds

support and is a threat to surge forward or hit penetrating balls. Both outside

wingbacks offer wide options to get in and behind the defense. The movement shown

is just one example of the many possible movement patterns. The creative

interchanging of positions during attack in the 4-2-3-1 is one of the main attributes of

the system.

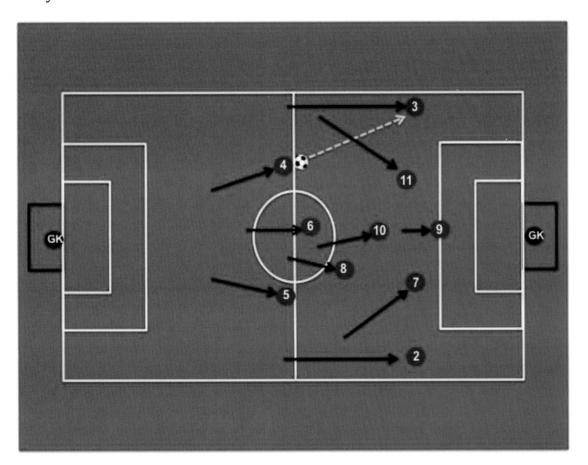

Building From The Back

4-2-3-1

Five Basic Options

Option #1: Center backs split creating space for the defensive center midfield player to drop and receive the ball side on. Notice how high the wingbacks are pushed up the field from a goal kick. This will open the field up and force the opponents to adjust. However, opening the field extremely wide is often better for highly skilled and technical teams. Once the #6 receives the ball, the #8 should present a diagonal forward passing option on an angle. The #6 should have many options available at various distances to choose from. Notice the amount of triangles and diamonds that are present in this set-up for passing options. The general rule when working the ball out of the defensive third is to not play too many passes in row up the middle. Teams who give the ball away in the middle of their own defensive third are very susceptible to the quick counter.

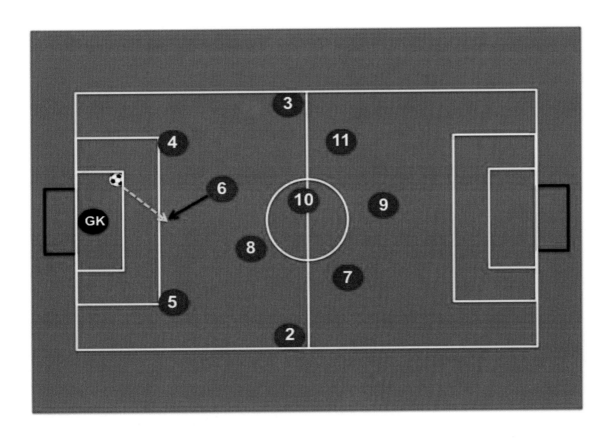

Option #2: From the goal kick, the #3 wingback has dropped deep to the end line and wide. The left center back #4 has pinched towards the center to create space. Once the ball is played to #3 the #6 can check into the available space presenting a passing option. Teams that drop deeper may elect not to extend pressure to player#3 at all. The deep drop by player#3 will give him more time on the ball.

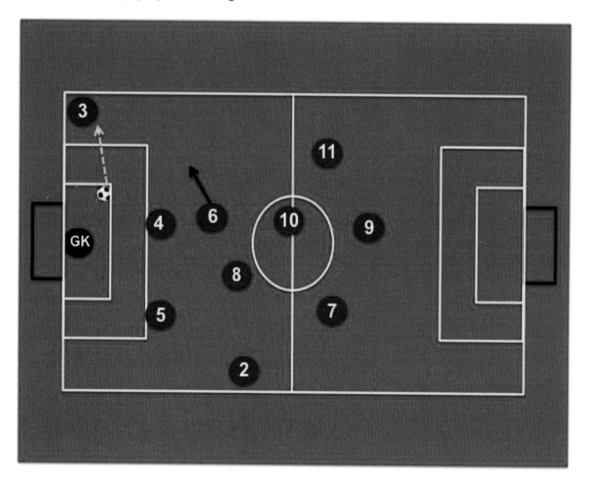

Option#3: Both center backs shift over to one side of the box creating space on left side for #6 to check into the space to receive the ball. It is important that the #6 comes from a deeper position and makes his run at speed into the space to receive the ball side on. The #6 must always be scanning the field and know if there is pressure over his shoulder. The worst thing that can happen on the top of the box is to turn the ball over carelessly, because the player on the ball did not realize there was pressure.

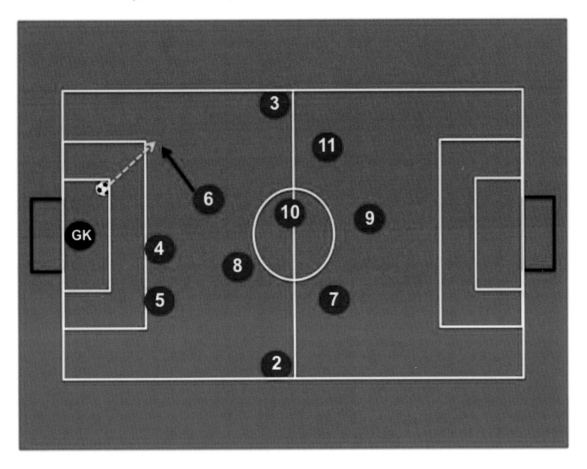

Option#4: The Center Back will drop all the way to the end line to receive the pass. This is similar to option#2, but this time it is the center back dropping deep. Most opposing teams will not expect the center back to drop and it may catch them off guard.

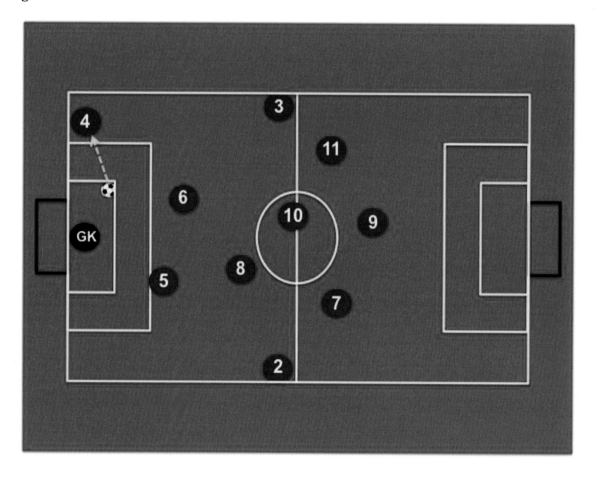

Option#5: If the opposing team is pressing high up the field, a longer pass should be considered. Teams that play a 4-3-3 and look to press 3 players high would be a good example of this. In this diagram the keeper picks out a second line pass to the wingback relieving the pressure and by passing and defenders that were pressing high.

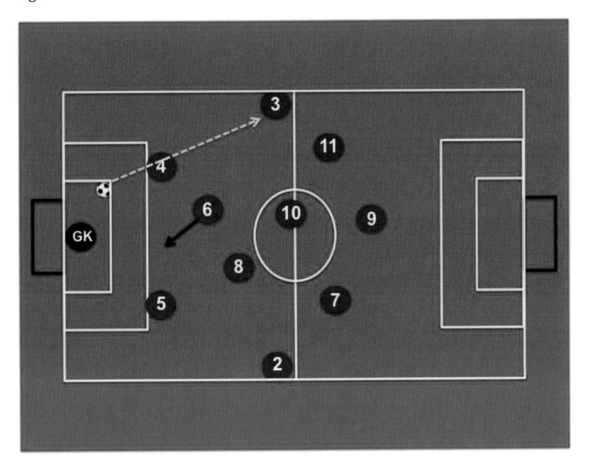

Collective Team Movement Patterns in Possession

The Defensive & Middle Thirds

4-2-3-1

The coach can customize player's roles and responsibilities within the 4-2-3-1 formation to fit the desired game plan. For example, the coach would dictate if the center backs should play slightly wider or more narrow in possession (playing more narrow to guard against the counter) or instructing how high the wingbacks should advance forward when building up possession out of the back (opening up to much leaves gaps the opponents can exploit in transition). An experienced high-level team may elect to push their wingbacks all the way to half field and wide on a goal kick, while a less skilled team may only push them up 15 yards from the penalty box. All of these parameters are set by the coach and directly affect the way the 4-2-3-1 is played. Here are two examples of movement patterns that can be used for working the ball out of the defensive and middle thirds out of the field.

Example One

The center backs start to widen making room for the #6. The #8 provides a

forward diagonal option for the #6, serving as a link to get the ball forward or wide.

The wingbacks #3 & #2 provide width as they advance up the field, coordinating their

movements with the wingers #11 & #7.

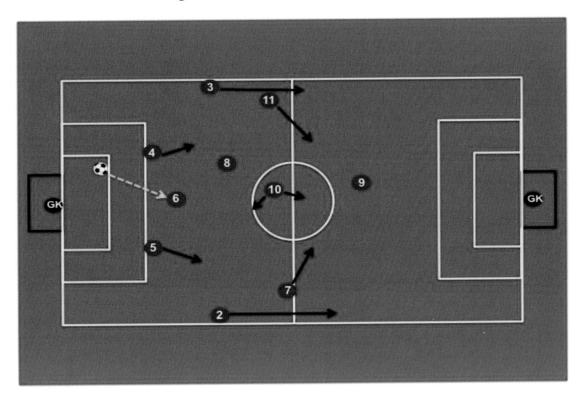

Example Two

The wingback #2 elects to under lap as the winger #7 stays wide. The #9 runs diagonally into space as the #10 surges forward and #7 runs the flank. This type of coordinated movement is very effective, presents problems for the defense and creates attacking overloads in dangerous areas of the field. Notice the wingback #3 & winger #11 have the opposite movement of #2 and #7.

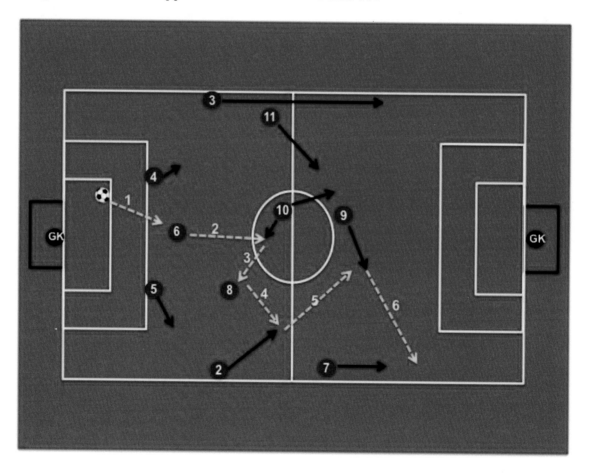

Color Coded Partnerships

4-2-3-1

Color-coding the players in pairs can help them understand how the 4-2-3-1

formation works. The coordination and understanding of movements between the

pairs must be excellent. Notice when the #7 & #11 cuts in the #2 & #3 will take up

the open space. The #10 & #9 will often interchange positions taking up the space

each has left for each other. Using color-coded shadow play in training is a great way

for players to learn movement options. A full 11 v 11 training game can also be

played color-coded, have the opposite team wear a non-conflicting solid color.

Watching the color-coded team's movements will be easy for the coach and players to

identify. Color-coded training can be applied to a variety of exercises in this book.

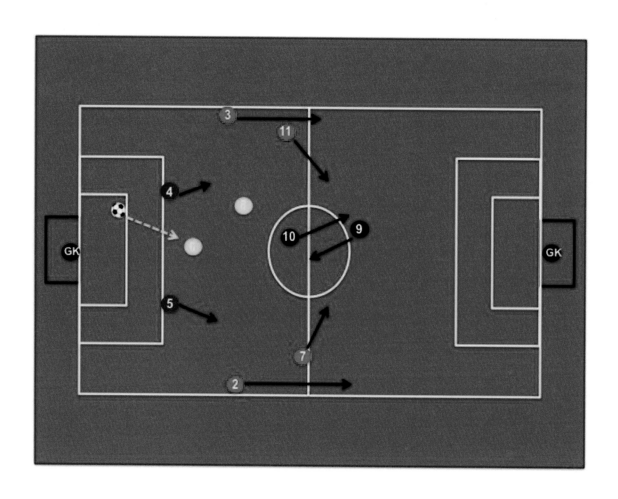

Playing Out of The Back & Middle Thirds

Training Exercises

Exercise 1: Coordinated Movement:

.....In this exercise the ball will start with the goalkeeper. Each player will start on their indicated cone. Once #6 receives the ball on the half turn, looks forward and lifts his head ready to pass the ball, the players on the cones will perform their coordinated movements. The #6 will be free to pass to whichever player he wants to. The ball must be passed to every color once. When each color has touched the ball it will be sent back to the keeper. The keeper will then restart the sequence. The #6 should mix up distribution from left to right. The main goal is to get the players to move together at the correct time only after #6 is ready to pass the ball. Timing of movement is everything.

Variation:

In this example, notice the varied movement of the #10 & #9 along with the movement of #2 & 7. The #2 will initially tuck back towards the #5 when seeing the #6 is facing the opposite direction looking to play the ball. When the #8 receives the ball the #7 could sprint diagonally towards the middle as the #2 would then push down the sideline. The idea is to have players run only when the player on the ball can see them and realistically pass them the ball. Running at the wrong time will destroy possession, take away passing options and make teams defensively vulnerable when possession is lost.

Feel free to create various patterns. After the team executes the pattern you may have them continue down the field and improvise until they finish on goal.

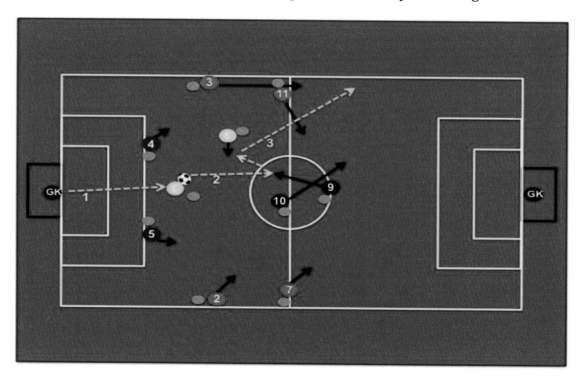

Exercise 2 - Ajax FC Playing Out of The Back:

The purpose of the training is to practice working the ball out of the back effectively.

The blue team is lined up using a 4-1-2, while the red team is playing a 3-1-2

formation. The example shows the center backs splitting and the #6 looking to collect

the ball. If the red team decided to push 3 players to pressure the blue #4, 5 & 6, the

keeper would look to play either blue wingback (#2 or #3). When teams press high

the longer option should be used to bypass the pressure of the pressing front players.

I like this drill because it allows for many meaningful repetitions working the ball out

of the back. The movement patterns can be put into play under realistic game related

circumstances.

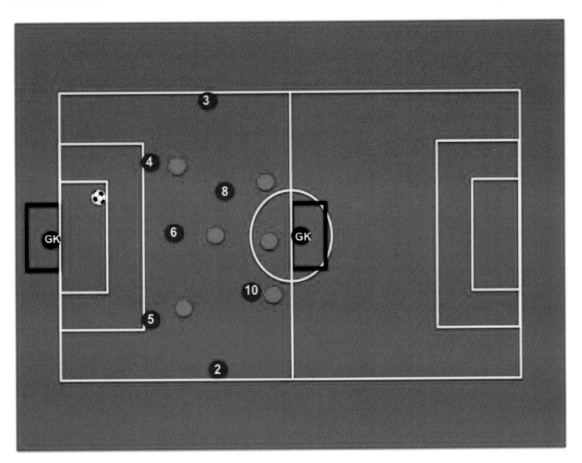

Exercise 3 - Arsenal FC – Playing out of the Back - 7 v 5

The blue team of 7 players is trying to score one of the two smaller goals. The ball starts with the keeper as the blue team attempts to build possession out of the back. The blue team is restricted to 2-touch, as they focus on opening up the field and circulating the ball. If the red team wins possession, they have a maximum of 4 passes to shoot. By making red team shoot within 4 passes, it keeps the majority of the training focused on the blue team, so they can train working the ball out of the back. The drill provides realistic and meaningful repetitions for the blue team with the objective of working the ball out of the back.

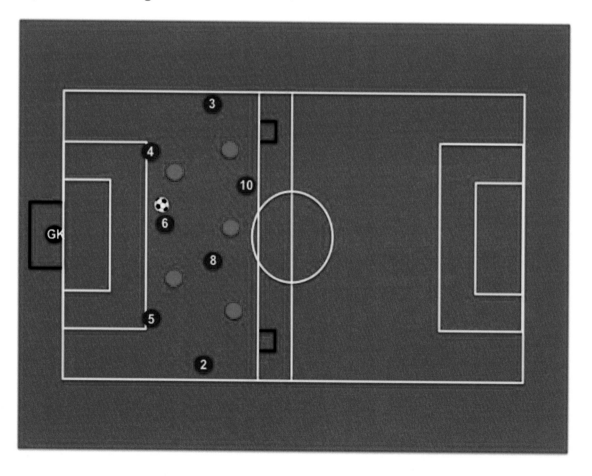

Exercise 4 - Goal to Zone: 11 v 8

The blue team will score on the 7-yard zone that runs across the field (marked by the red lines). In order to score, the blue player must pass the ball into the 7-yard zone to a teammate that times his run into the zone and stops the ball. Blue players are not allowed to dribble into the zone or wait in the zone to receive a pass. The red team scores on the keeper and regular goal. Blue is limited to 2-touch play, while the red players are allowed unlimited touches. This drill was used often by Carlo Ancelotti at Chelsea FC and PSG in France. The exercise is game realistic and focuses on building possession out of the defensive and middle thirds.

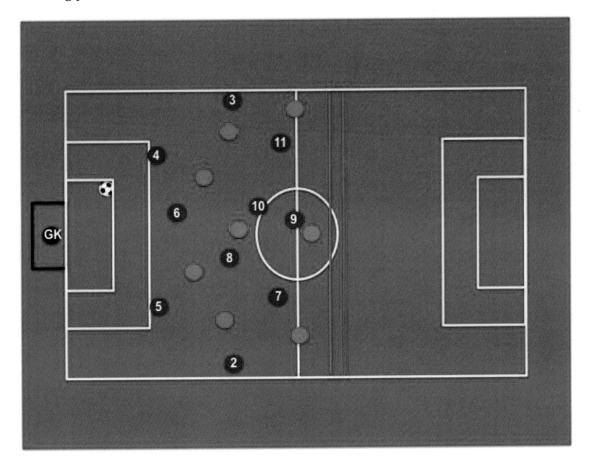

Exercise 5 - Goal to Zone: 11v10

This drill is the progression from 11v8 exercise - it provides full pressure opposition for the blue team to train against.

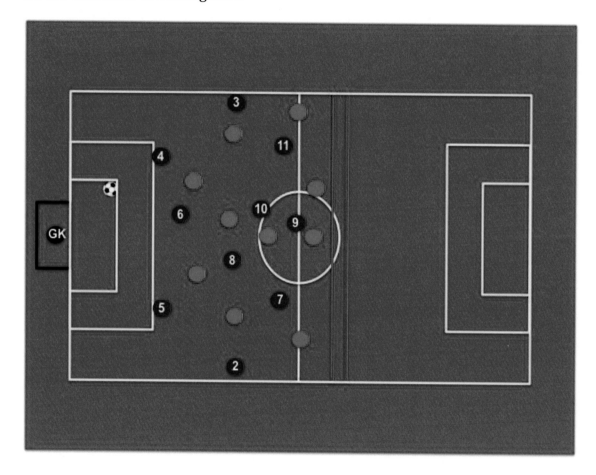

Exercise 6 - Shadow Play: 11 v 0 - 11 v 7

True shadow play is without opposition. Teams will pass the ball down the field as a unit with the end result being a shot on goal. It is important to make the attacking movement as game realistic as possible (even with no opposition). Eventually, I like to add defenders to the shadow play. I build up a few players at a time, until around 7 defenders are being used. If the defending team intercepts the ball, play starts with the team of 10 working the ball from the keeper. When training shadow play make sure the teams movement and rhythm of passing is realistic. The coach can encourage this by giving instructions to switch the field, play the ball back, attack wide, attack central, wingback overlaps and more. The team will have to react to the coach's commands and adjust accordingly. I picked up an interesting variation of shadow play from Professional Coach Tony Waiters a few years back. He would run two teams at one time attacking opposite goals doing shadow play. The teams would have to avoid each other on the field as they both intertwine passing the ball moving towards their respected goals. I use two-team shadow play often with my own teams to train patterns and teach coordinated team movements.

Shadow Play:

The blue team carries out attacking movements and finishes on the far goal.

Eventually the coach can add defenders to make the exercise more challenging. I

suggest starting with 3 defenders and building to a maximum of 7.

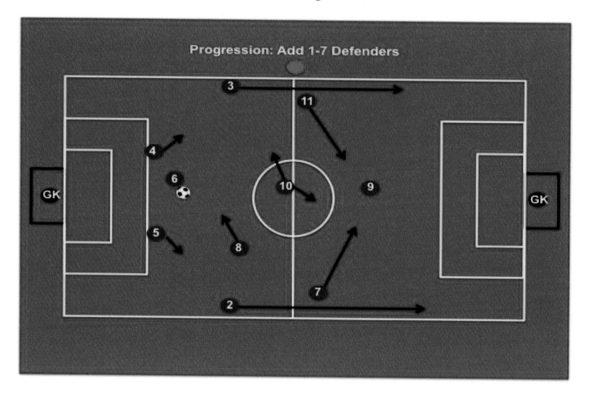

Two Team Shadow Play:

The blue team is working the ball one direction as the red team is working the opposite direction. The objective is to have both teams carry out their attacking movements ending with a shot on goal.

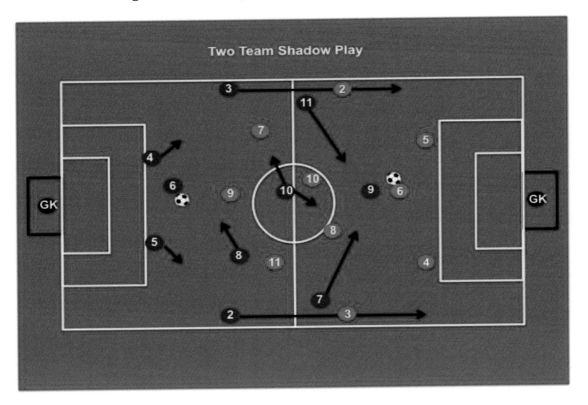

Movement Patterns In The Middle and Attacking Thirds

4-2-3-1

Sample Patterns: Movement in soccer is dynamic, as players pick up cues that indicate what spaces to run into and when. Effective team movement requires intelligent well-timed coordinated runs into space. Movement patterns are useful in giving players options & ideas. The overall strategy of the team will be reflected in the movement and set up of the players. The movement patterns shown below serve to provide just a few ideas of possible collective team movement in the attacking third. It is important to remember that movement off the ball is 90% of the game or more. In order to be effective, movement off the ball must be executed at the right time. Moving too early or too late is not effective and will result in wasted running with no purpose. If you ever have the opportunity to watch Spain or Barcelona from a stadium view, you will notice something right away about movement patterns. Wherever the ball is, there is coordinated well-timed movement between 2-4 players. The rest of the team is not running round the field, they are waiting. As the ball moves the players around the ball start to move, forming triangles and diamonds. Eventually, when the ball is being passed around in the triangles, a penetrating run through or out wide will happen to unlock the defense. Movement patterns in the 4-2-3-1 vary according to the style of play as well. The 4-2-3-1 that Manchester City plays will look much different than the same formation played by Barcelona. Teams like Manchester City or Liverpool use a more direct approach to the game but are still very effective. The style of play, which is directly dictated by the team tactics and skill level, will determine the movement patterns to some extent. If a team sits deep and counters, their movement patterns will be much different than a team committed to dominating possession. The 4-2-3-1 can be used effectively to counter or possess, the way it is played is up to the coach. Remember, every soccer game is different so adjustments may be needed to get the most out of your team and system. The only way to make smart adjustments is to educate your self and study the formation (all formations really).

Pattern One:

The interchanging of positions and freedom of movement in the 4-2-3-1 is a major part of its effectiveness. The wingbacks main job is to provide width in the attack, allowing the wingers to cut inside. If the winger stays wide the wingback can cut inside on an underlap. In this example the wingbacks #2 & #3 push forward and the wingers #11 & #7 cut inside forming a diamond shape in the middle with players #9 & #10. This shape is very attack minded and creates many attacking overload opportunities. However, with so many players committed forward it leaves the attacking team open to a counter attack down the outside channels. To make the team shape less vulnerable to the counter-the opposite side wingback would not push forward as aggressively. Instead, he would wait until the ball is switched back to the middle of the field to a player who was looking to play down his side. The central player would have eye contact with his head up looking to play into space. This would be the cue for the wingback to make the run fast, taking up the wide attacking space. The #9 and #10 are free to interchange positions as shown. The #8 finds a balance between attack and supporting the attack. The #6 operates as the deepest midfield player swinging the ball from side to side switching the field. The center backs stay put but there will be a few opportunities a game that space opens for one of them to come forward with the ball (this can be risky and only done when the opponents are playing one forward and allowing lots of space).

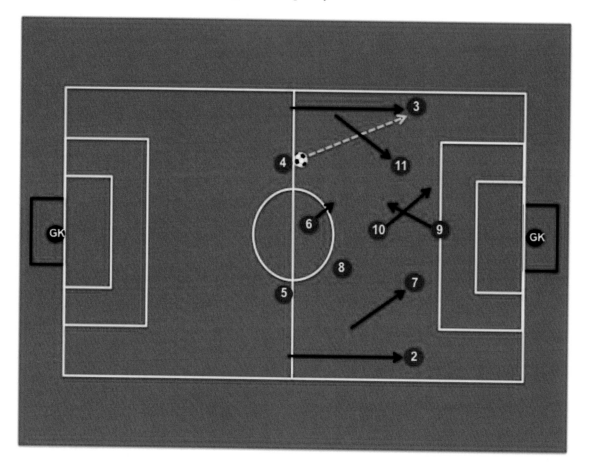

Pattern Two:

This pattern shows the wingback #3 underlapping as the winger #11 stays high and wide. Once the #3 has the ball the #11 could look to cut inside for a through ball from #3. In this example, the opposite side winger makes a cross field run exploiting the spaces between the center back and right back forcing the defense to problem solve. The wingback #2 pushes into the space the #7 has left and provides attacking width.

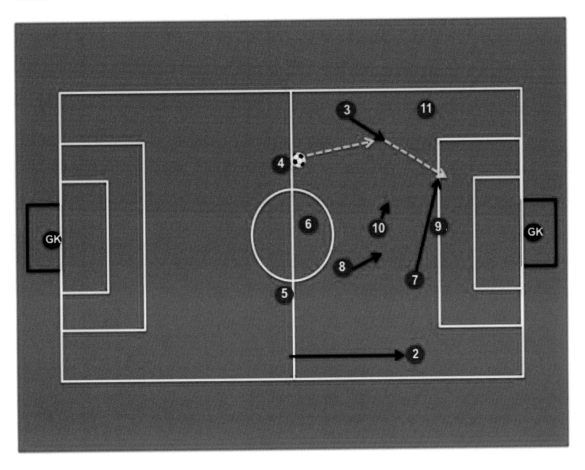

Pattern Three:

This pattern shows the #9 looking to exploit space between the center back and the

right back. The #10 will fill the space left by the #9. The wingers cut in as the

wingbacks provide width and depth out wide.

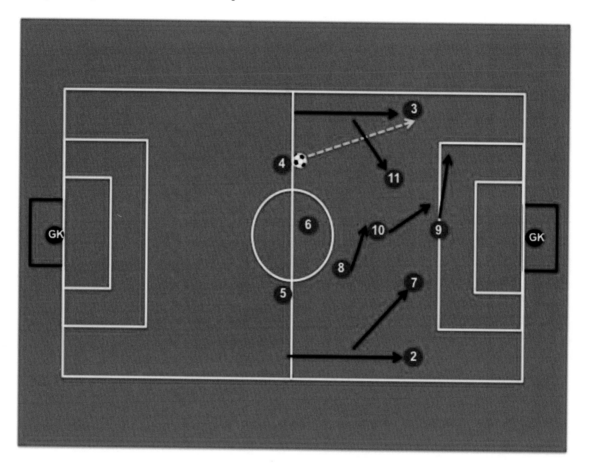

Attacking Play In The Middle & Final Third

Training Exercises

4-2-3-1

These training exercises are designed to create game realistic attacking play while playing the 4-2-3-1.

Exercise One: 6v6 Phase Play

The red team is trying to score on the keeper while the blue team is looking to score on either small goal. The red team will be encouraged to interchange movements when in possession. In order to keep the focus on the red attacking team, the blue team must score within 5 or fewer passes after a turnover. The red team is set-up position specific to the 4-2-3-1.

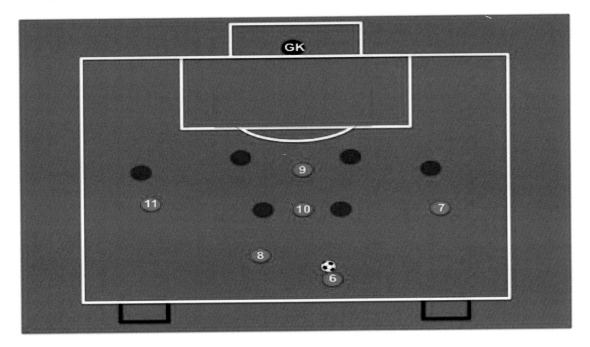

Exercise Two: 6v6 Zone 14 Phase Play

There is now a square grid marked out in front of the back four. This is called "Zone 14". Zone 14 is the area between the back line and the midfielders. Attackers who can pick the ball up in this space will be able to penetrate the defense by passing, shooting and even dribbling. Players that play in between the lines of the opponents cause them many marking and team shape problems. In this exercise, only one red player at a time can enter inside the "Zone 14" box. The blue team is not allowed to enter inside the "Zone 14 Box". The red team is set up position specific to the 4-2-3-1. They will try to break the blue team and finish on goal. If the blue team gains possession they have 5 passes or fewer to score on the two small goals.

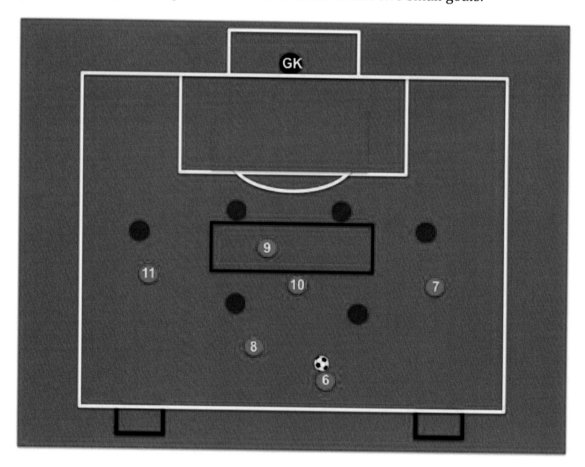

Exercise Three: 8v6, 8v7 & 8v8 Zone 14

This exercise is the same as exercise two, but the numbers progress to 8 v 6 - 8 v 8. The outside wingbacks are now included, adding width to the attack. Red scores on the keeper and blue has 5 passes or less to score on either of the small sided goals at midfield. Try the exercise with and without the "Zone 14".

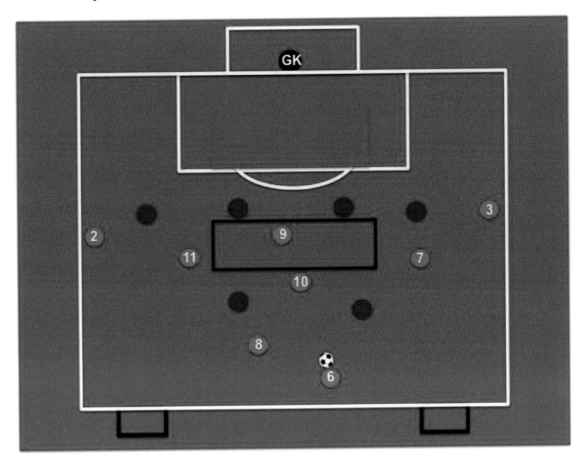

Exercise Four: 8v6, 8v7 & 8v8 Zonal Passing Play

In this phase play exercise, the red team is not allowed to hit a straight forward pass. Each forward pass must be hit diagonally into another lane (passes that go forward can be hit to the next lane over, but the pass must be forward on an angle). Red players can only play back diagonally into a different lane. Square balls must skip an entire lane. As a variation you can allow a forward straight ball, if the player you are passing to runs into the lane to receive it (they can't be standing stationary & they must come running from another lane). This exercise gets players thinking about movement, angles and supporting runs.

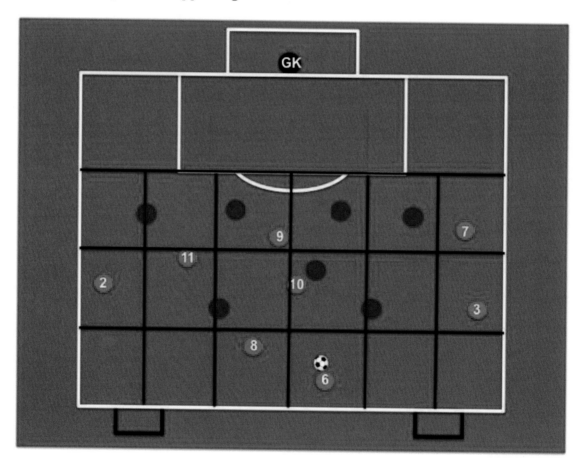

Exercise Five: 11 v 9 Wingers Both Ways

The winger's who are wearing red, play for the team in possession. This will create attacking overloads for the team in possession (11 v 9), especially out wide. The defending team will need to recover quickly after losing possession. Encourage the team in possession to not give the ball away easily and use the numerical advantage to breakdown the defending team by creating attacking overloads.

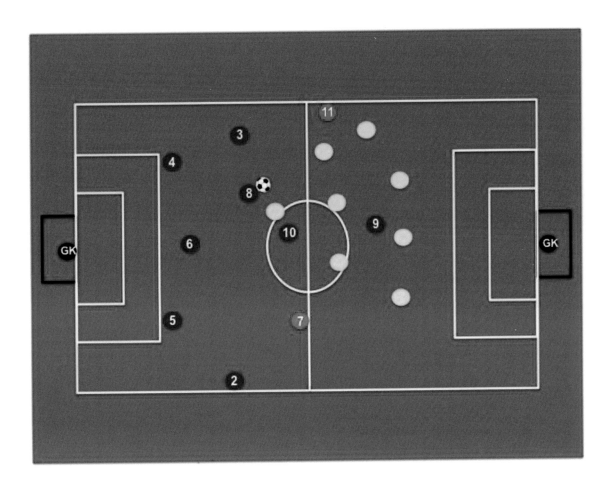

Exercise Six: #10 Both Ways

This training exercise is similar to exercise five. The difference is the #10 in red plays with the team in possession of the ball. This will create an attacking overload in center of the midfield. Building the attack through the middle to exploit the central overload should be encouraged.

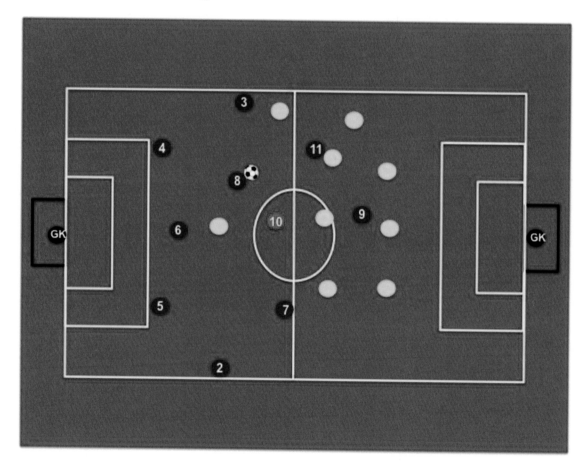

Exercise Seven: Arsenal Attacking Third

The blue team will attack the red team looking to score on goal in the attacking third. The only player allowed to sit in the middle third is the defensive center midfielder #6 for blue. If the red team steals the ball from the blue team, they will attack the yellow team. If the blue team scores on the red team, they will start a new ball and attack the yellow team.

The idea of the drill is break down a team that sits. It encourages ball circulation, movement off the ball and creativity in order to break down the 8 players that are sitting deep. Make sure the players are assigned the specific roles from the 4-2-3-1 formation.

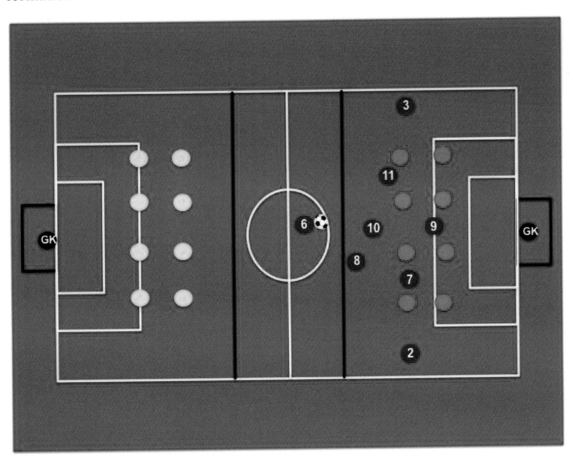

Exercise Eight: 8v8v8 Rapid Attack

This rapid moving exercise works on attacking movement and speed of the counter attack. Attacking teams start by taking on the shape shown by the blue team. The positions played will be identical to the roles of 4-2-3-1(without the center backs). Encourage movement and the interchanging of positions in attack.

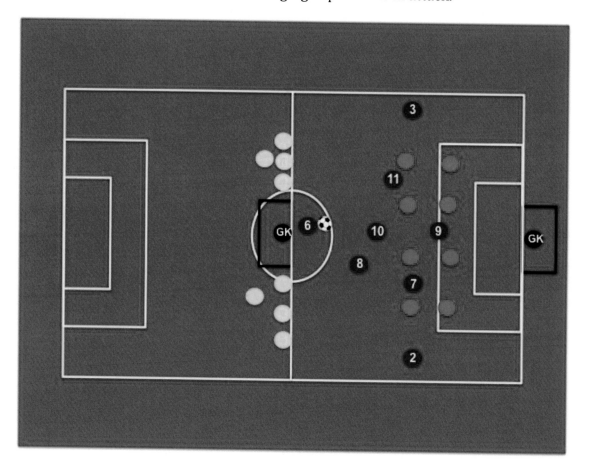

Exercise Nine: Midfield Box

This 11 v 11 game incorporates a 2-touch box (for more skilled players this can be a 1-touch box). Players outside the box have unlimited touches. Players are free to move inside and outside of the box interchanging positions. The 2-touch or 1-touch box speeds play up in the midfield and forces support to be given in the wide areas.

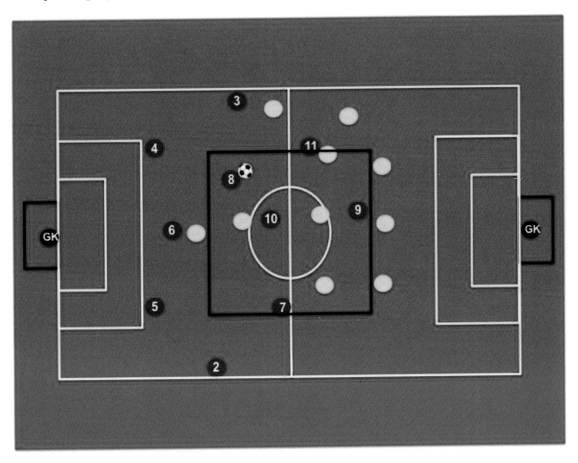

Exercises Ten: Two-Team Shadow Play

The blue team attacks one goal moving the ball down the field as the red team does the same attacking the other goal. The teams must be aware and avoid each other while executing their attacking movements passing the ball. After each team finishes on goal, they will jog back to the other side of the field and build a new attack. Emphasize coordinated movement, passing the ball to all lines, establishing a good passing rhythm, demanding constant communication between players and finishing each attacking movement with a quality shot on goal. Two-team shadow play is an effective way to teach movement for any system of play.

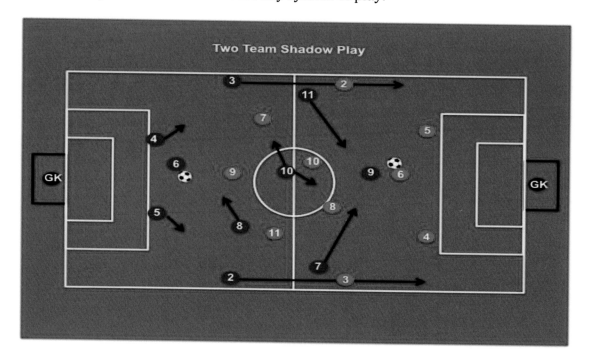

Exercise Eleven: 3-2-1-Touch

This 11 v 11 game is played full field using the width of the penalty box. The compact field makes movement and finding space difficult for the attacking team. The smaller space will force players to be even sharper and more coordinated in their movement off the ball. Play 5 minutes 3-touch, 5 minutes 2-touch and 5 minutes 1-touch.

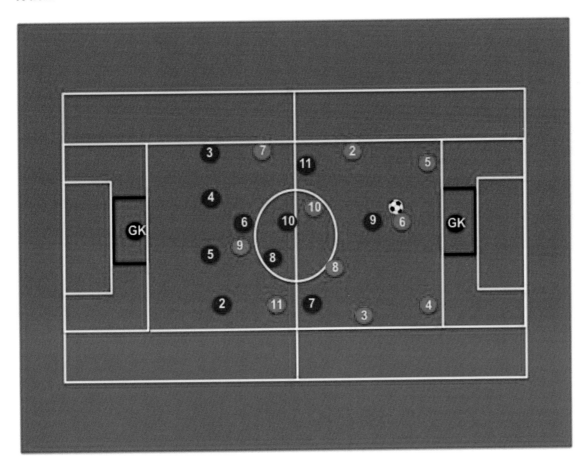

Exercise Twelve: One Zone

This 11 v 10 game uses a zone and a goal to score on. The blue team will score by passing the ball to a player running into the 7-yard zone. The red team will be scoring on the regular sized goal. The blue team scoring on the cross-field zone will be able to exploit the red team if they use effective movement off the ball. The zone is much harder to defend than the goal because of the size of the zone. Teams should look to create attacking overloads to breakdown the defending team. The teams must be set-up in the 4-2-3-1 formation.

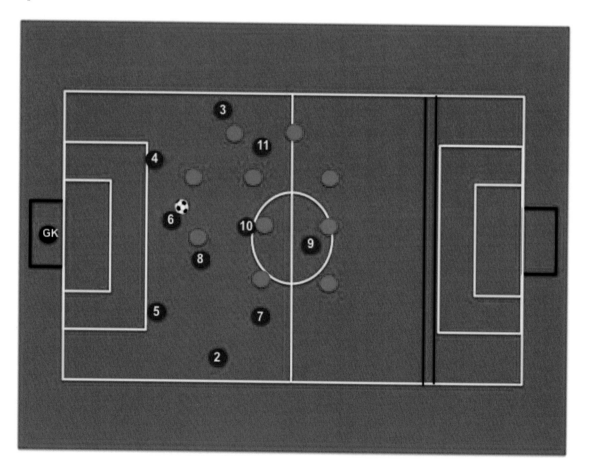

Exercise Thirteen: Two Zone

This 10 v 10 game uses two cross field zones similar to exercise eleven. Teams score by passing the ball into the 7-yard zone to a teammate who is running into the zone and stops the ball. Because both zones are so wide, breaking down the defending team is possible with almost every possession (although it obviously will not happen in every possession). Attacking overloads should be created to break down the defending team. Make sure the formation and roles of the 4-2-3-1 are maintained.

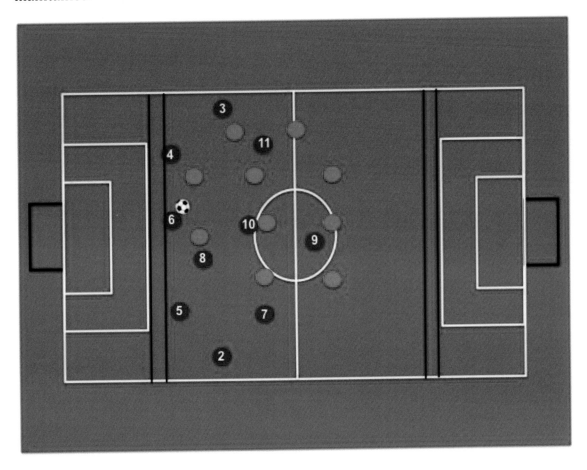

Defending In The 4-2-3-1

The defensive strategy will shape the way the entire game is played. If a team commits to sit deep and counter attack, they have committed to allowing the majority of possession to go to the opposing team. This means for the majority of the game there will be 40-60 yards open behind the opponent's back four which is available to exploit. Sitting deeper and counter attacking is becoming more prominent in the modern game. Teams like Liverpool, Chelsea and Manchester City have experienced great success playing this way. In order to be effective playing the counter, teams must attack with speed, be very accurate in their forward passing and try to get a couple of players pushing forward to assist in the attacking movement (1-3 players on a counter attack is sufficient most times). The 4-2-3-1 works very well on the counter attack and is defensively very sound, especially when sitting deep. To make things simple I will suggest three ways to play defense in the 4-2-3-1. Each option will bring about a much different effect on the game.

Full Press:

The full press is a commitment to press extremely high up the field and force the opponent to turn the ball over in their own attacking third. This pressure will disrupt or destroy the opponent's ability to work the ball out of the back. In order to press effectively, players must understand angles, take away spaces, work collectively, have a high fitness level and play with the proper mentality and toughness. A team that executes a press well can control games. The danger of pressing high is the space that will open up behind the back four. If the opposing team breaks the press, the pressing team will be extremely vulnerable with less numbers to defend and 50 yards of space behind the back four. One through ball at this point can result in a 1v1 breakaway. In the diagram below, the red line indicates the line of confrontation and the blue line marks the line of restraint.

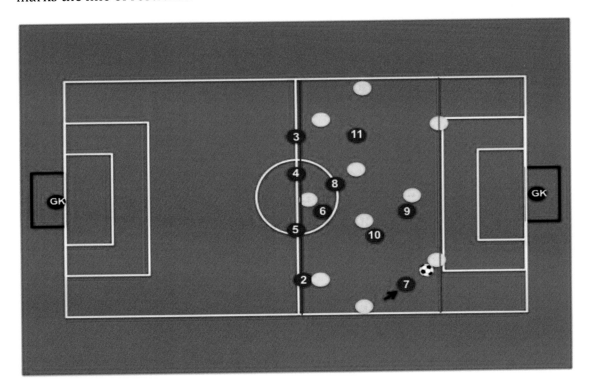

Half Press:

Notice the adjustment of the line of confrontation (red line) and the line of restraint (blue line), they are moved much further back in the half press. These lines dictate the shape of the team. However, players can extend pressure over the line of confrontation in groups of 1-3 players. Extending pressure puts the opponents under pressure and does not allow them hit non-pressured passes that pick apart the defense. Extending pressure often results in creating turnovers as well. The forward is the only player that is almost always located above the line of confrontation. The forward#9 will cut out passing options to the center backs and even help trap the wingbacks.

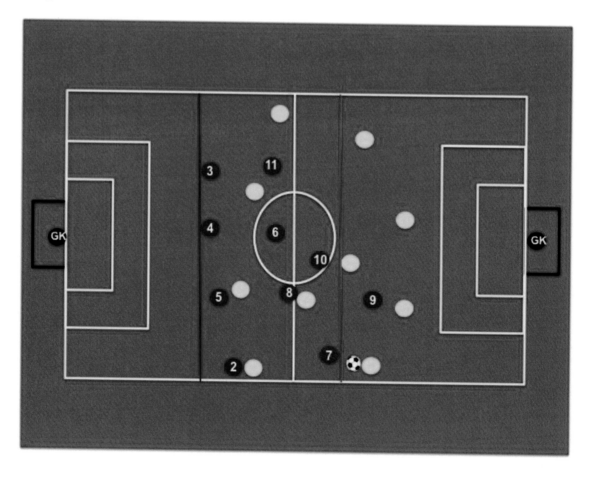

Dropping Deep:

Notice how deep the line of confrontation is now. There is little space to be exploited behind the defending teams back line. This is a particular good strategy when playing against teams whose forwards are very fast. Sitting this deep naturally gives the defending team a more compact shape that is harder to breakdown. Playing deep is perfect for a counter-attacking style in the 4-2-3-1. However, in order to counter attack 1-4 players must break once possession is gained. The forward passing and movement off the ball by the countering players must be efficient, direct and into space. When teams decide to sit they must be content with the opponent's controlling possession of the ball. The coach can elect to sit his team deep for the entire game or use the tactic when needed. For example: sitting deep the last 10 minutes of the game to kill the game off and protect the lead.

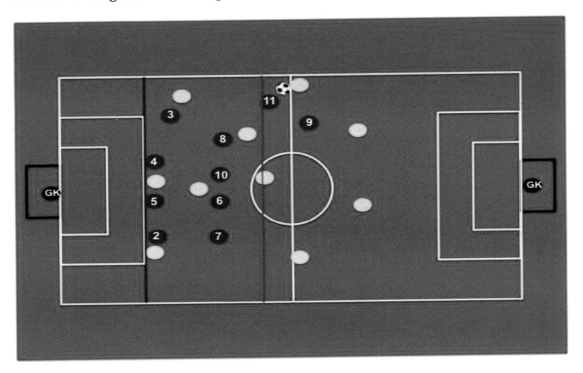

4-2-3-1 Defensive Responsibilities

I wanted to touch briefly on the general marking responsibilities of players in the system. The wingers #7 & #11 will be responsible for marking the attacking outside fullbacks or wingbacks. The forward #9 will stop the center back from coming forward with the ball, cut off the fullbacks or wingbacks option to play the ball to the center back and, if possible, work with the winger to trap the opposing team's fullback in possession. The #9 can only be so many places as the lone forward, so the responsibilities need to be realistic. However, a high work rate is needed out of the forward. The days of the forward walking around and not contributing defensively are over. The forward needs to work hard on defense and possess the fitness to have full energy to attack as well.

The rotation at midfield may be the most important to figure out in the system. I prefer to split the responsibilities into zones for the #6,8 and 10 to share. Splitting the area up into three zones makes covering the large midfield space easier for the players. I do not have the #6 just sit and not move in front of the center backs. My #6 does cover some space and the #8 covers for the #6 if he is pulled out of position. The diagram shows how I break down those zones in the center midfield.

Center Midfield Zones of Responsibility:

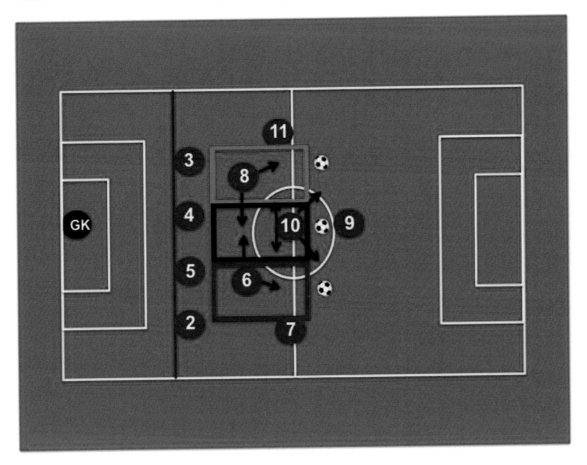

4-2-3-1 Defending Training Sessions

Exercise One: 6 v 4

This is a standard exercise that works on the coordination of the back 4 defenders. It is always good to start with the back and build to the midfield when teaching defending. The red team attacks and tries to score on goal as the blue team works together as a unit to defend (offside rule applies). If the blue team gains possession they will clear the ball to one of the two neutral players standing at midfield.

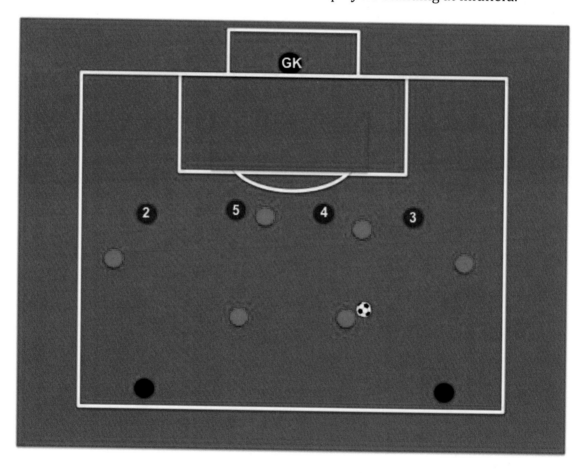

Exercise Two: 8 v 6

This is the next progression from Exercise One. Two defensive center midfield players are added to provide a screen in front of the back four. The two blue center midfielders should not be pulled out into wide areas. They need to stay compact and guard the center of the field. The red team should be set-up with two wide players, two forwards, two center midfielders and two players that sit back and swing the ball from side to side. If the blue team gains possession, they will clear the ball to one of the two neutral players standing at midfield. Offside rules does apply. This is exercise has now progressed to a 4-2 formation on defense that is realistic to the actual 4-2-3-1 formation.

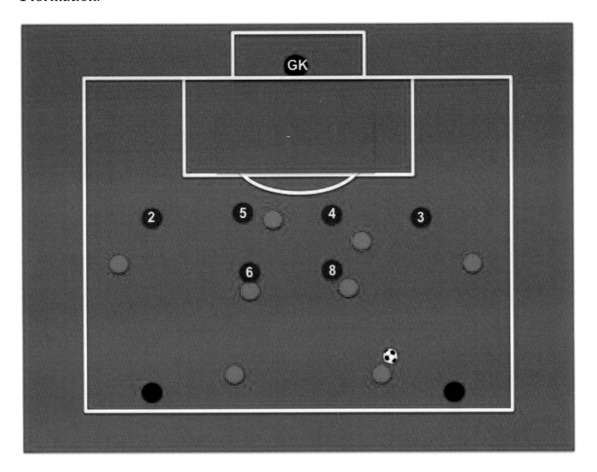

Exercise Three: 10 v 8

This is the final progression of the drill. The blue team is defending with two lines of 4 players as the red team is playing with all 10 players. The same rules apply from the previous progressions.

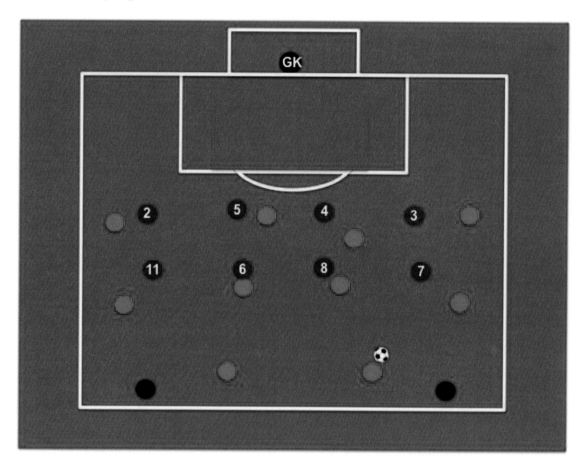

Exercise Four: Full Press, Half Press & Dropping Deep: 11 v 11

This exercise is an 11 v 11 full field game. The blue team will be instructed which line to hold by the coach. The coach will change the line frequently forcing the blue team to adjust their defending and attacking tactics. It is important for players to be able to go from dropping back to pressing in a short time period. Mentally, players find it difficult to switch from sitting to pressing sometimes. If the coach trains this in practice the players will be better adjusted to execute in the games. Feel free to arrange the yellow team in different formations in order to make the blue team problem solve.

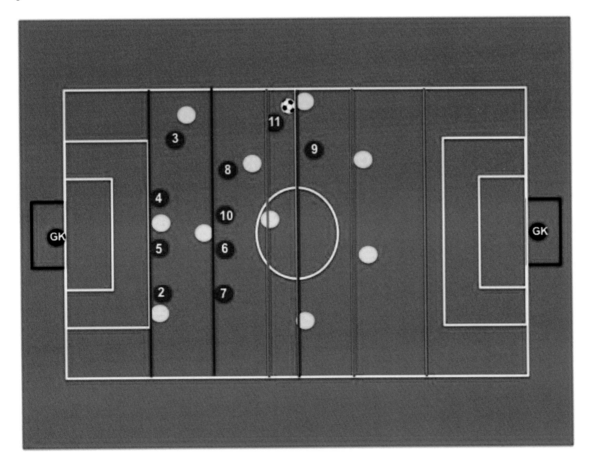

4-2-3-1 Creating Overloads

The below example is the 4-2-3-1 against a 4-4-2 Diamond. When the field is divided into grids it makes understanding overloads and match-ups easier. Take a look at the boxes and see where the numerical advantages are for the blue team. Once you add movement to the players the overloads change quickly. It is important for coaches and players to be able to recognize where the overloads are and how to create them. Each formation that you play against can be broken down to figure out the strengths and the weaknesses of each. Soccer is a free flowing game and is not as easy as it looks on chalkboard. However, the fundamental ideas and principles will hold true. Players who understand the fundamentals and tactics will be better suited to make adjustments and solve problems on the field.

The reality is both players and coaches most be great instant problem solvers in order to be successful. Eventually, with enough training the regular game should start to look like training grids to your players. They will be able to see the overload possibilities and exploit them all over the field.

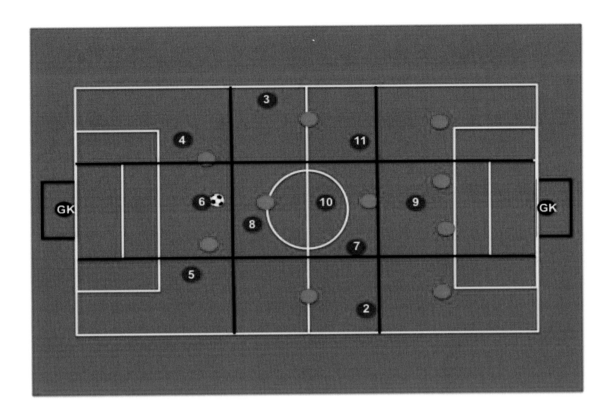

Adjusting & Modifying The 4-2-3-1

What happens if you are 2 goals up, 1 goal down, tied, man-up or man-down? All these situations will need to be addressed along with many more. My own personal philosophy is not to mess too much with the system. Going to three at midfield when we are used to five can be too much to ask. I prefer to make adjusts within the system that do not alter my player's thinking and habits drastically. If we are down a goal, one option is to have one or both wingers stay higher and not track as far back while defending. Playing a 4-4-2 is always a good option as well. Simply push another player up top, which might be the #10 being told to stay high and not come back to defend. This will leave two players high with eight to defend. The #6 and #8 would now have to split the field and share the defensive duty between the two.

The coach must think through all the possible adjustments and match it up with the personnel. Practice all the adjustments, scenarios and mentality's needed to play different ways in training.

Summary

Thanks for reading the book and I hope it has shed some light on playing the 4-2-3-1. I have used this system with my college team for many years with great success. Each season I continue analyze, reflect and learn new ways to make it better. If you have any questions feel free to email at coachdibernardo@gmail.com If you have not checked out any of my other books they are all available on Amazon. The books are a collection of the entire soccer curriculum I use on daily basis and complement each other in a cohesive interchangeable manner.

Other Books by:

The Method - The Art of Coaching & Managing Soccer

Soccer Smart

The Science of Rondo - Progressions, Variations and Transitions

45 Professional Soccer Possession Drills: Top Drills From The World's Top Clubs

Professional Soccer Restarts: 15 Corner Kicks that Work

Professional Soccer Restarts: 20 Free Kicks That Work

Professional Soccer Finishing Drills

Professional Soccer Passing Patterns

The Science of Soccer Team Defending

Cognitive Soccer Passing Patterns & Exercises: Developing Players Technical Ability,

Problem Solving Skills & Soccer IQ

Made in the USA
Columbia, SC
07 April 2019